## Plan with Purpose:
## A Business Journal for Women

A small business goal-setting writing journal for women who want to start a profitable business.

ISBN: 978-1-7357538-1-2
First Edition
Copyright © 2021 by Sincerely, Angie

All rights reserved. No part of this book may be reproduced, transferred, distributed or transmitted in any form which should include photocopying, scanning, recording or any other electronic methods without the prior written permission of the Publisher. Doing so would be in direct violation of the copyrights of the publisher, author and book. Permitted use include brief quotations for noncommercial use permitted by copyright law. Purchasing, reading or any use of and access to this book, grants you full access to the information exclusively for your personal use only.

Publisher
Sincerely, Angie
www.sincerelyangie.com

Printed in U.S.A
All imagery are licensed and/or copyright of Sincerely, Angie and remain the property of Sincerely, Angie. Every effort has been made to properly reference respective owners of all quotes, terms and copyrighted material accordingly, however, if there are any omissions, if made apparent, the Publisher will gladly revise the text to reflect such revelation in future reprints of this book.

The information herein is intended for your general knowledge and/or educational purposes only. The information herein is presented in good faith and is focused on providing reliable information on the forthcoming topic (s). Considerable efforts have been made to collect and publish reliable and readily available information, however, the Publisher and author disclaim responsibility and assume no liability for the validity of information contained herein or consequences for its use, misuse, or abuse. It is to be made apparent, the author and publisher are not required to render qualified services or represent such professionals such as a business consultant, accountant, attorney or financial professional.

The information in this book is based upon a combination of personal experiences from the author and consulting outside sources (i.e. local federal and state agencies). The advice presented herein may not be suited for your current business journey; furthermore, this book is not intended to replace guidance or consultation from a business professional or financial expert.

The information provided herein should not serve as a substitution for professional advice from a certified business professional.

This book is intended to be utilized as a guide and assist you while on your entrepreneurial journey . The author and publisher and mentioned companies are not responsible or liable for any loss, damage or harm resulting from the use of such information/advice or any information in this text described herein.

In using this journal/ advice, you, the reader, agree to indemnify, defend and hold harmless Sincerely, Angie, its directors, respective officers, employees, consultants, agents, contributors and affiliates, from any and all claims, demands, third party claims, liability, losses, damages, punitive or incidental damages, damages for loss of use or profits, damage to goodwill or reputation, other intangibles or the cost of procurement of substitute items and services, failures, claims for personal, property, tax, legal or financial damage and/or costs (including, but not limited to, legal fees, lawsuits, judgments) arising from your use of this book.

## Property of:

_____

*future business name*

## Belongs to:

_____

*future business owner*

*"A BIG BUSINESS STARTS SMALL"*
RICHARD BRANSON

# TABLE OF CONTENTS

## I. PLANT THE SEED

| | |
|---|---:|
| *Idea Generation* | **9** |
| *Categorize Your Idea* | **13** |
| *Business Plan* | **14** |
| *Your Brand Identity* | **23** |

## II. DEVELOP THE PLAN

| | |
|---|---:|
| *Get Legal* | **33** |
| *Incorporate* | **34** |
| *Small business Startup Costs* | **41** |
| *Product Development* | **45** |
| *Creating Policies* | **59** |
| *Forms for Your Small Business* | **65** |

## III. OPEN FOR BUSINESS

| | |
|---|---:|
| *Product Launch Teaser* | **80** |
| *Cost Structure* | **81** |

## IV. THE GROWTH STAGE

| | |
|---|---:|
| *Looking Ahead* | **100** |
| *Resources* | **107** |
| *Note Taking* | **111** |

BRING YOUR VISION TO LIFE!

# TAKING
## YOUR BUSINESS IDEAS
#### IN YOUR HEAD

## FROM THIS

x

# TO THIS

**Welcome and Greetings**, to you! You are about to embark on an incredible entrepreneurial journey!

As a serial entrepreneur with a couple of failed businesses under my belt (I can laugh about it now 🙂 ), I know first hand the amount of time, energy and money it takes to start a small business.

This guided business journal is for the new entrepreneur. Those who want to start a small business but just don't know how. I am here to help! My goal is to push you forward on your entrepreneurial journey by helping you map out a concise business plan, avoid the countless mistakes that I made and create a profitable small business.

**Tough love alert**: This journal will *require* you to do *a lot* of work to create a tailored plan designed specially for you so be prepared to *work*.

Upon completion of this journal, you will have a clear idea of how to start a small business, one that you are passionate about. Are you ready?

Get excited about the journey. Trust the process. Document your progress. Most importantly, have fun!

Cheers, to a new beginning!

*Sincerely, Angie* ♥

# COMMITMENT CONTRACT

I, _____ , hereby agree and commit myself to achieving my business goals. My business goals are:

- 
- 
- 

By signing this contract, I signify that I have committed myself to achieving my business goals. I acknowledge that the journey will be hard but it will be worthwhile.

I also agree to complete this journal in its entirety.

Signature: _____

Date: _____

YOUR JOURNEY STARTS HERE

# SELF-DISCOVERY

## GETTING TO KNOW YOU

"The longest journey is the journey inward."
*Dag Hammarskjold*

## WHO ARE YOU?

List your interests and things that you are passionate about, things that motivate and inspire you, your purpose, values, etc. Also list who you are now and who you desire to be.

_____

_____

_____

_____

_____

## WHAT ARE YOUR SUPER POWERS?

List your strengths, talents and gifts.

_____

_____

_____

_____

_____

# WHY DO YOU WANT YOUR OWN BUSINESS?

List why you want to start your own business. Refer to your previous answers if needed.

_____

_____

_____

_____

_____

# WHERE ARE YOU NOW IN LIFE?

List your current stage in life. Are you single, married, retired, in school, etc.

_____

_____

_____

_____

_____

# HOW WILL YOU MAKE THIS YOUR PRIORITY?

List how you will manage your time, evaluate current priorities and commitments, etc.

_____

_____

_____

_____

_____

# WHEN DO YOU WANT TO START YOUR BUSINESS?

List your timeline for starting your small business. (Ex: Within the next year, after you get married, etc.)

_____

_____

_____

_____

_____

*Plant the seed and watch it grow.*

*The seeds you plant today will blossom into flowers tomorrow*

— SEE

*Harvest season is right around the corner.*

## *Idea Generator*

# 7 STREAMS OF INCOME

It is a well-known fact, that most millionaires have at least seven streams of income. Although these streams of income are produced from different sources, my goal is to get you to start thinking BIG. Let's begin the brainstorming session by exploring your top business ideas. Below, write down your top seven business ideas. First write down the industry and then your idea.

**1.** _____
_____
_____
_____

**2.** _____
_____
_____
_____

**3.** _____
_____
_____
_____

# Idea generator

♡♡♡♡♡♡♡♡  ♡♡♡♡♡♡♡♡

**4**
_____
_____
_____
_____

**5**
_____
_____
_____
_____

**6**
_____
_____
_____
_____

**7**
_____
_____
_____
_____

# CATEGORIZE IDEAS

Now that you have listed your top seven business ideas, you can now categorize each into the four categories below.

### EASY WINS
- FEASIBLE
- CLEAR OPPORTUNITIES
- YIELDS LOW OUTCOME

### HIGH PRIORITY
- FEASIBLE WITH FEW RESOURCES
- YIELDS HIGH OUTCOME

### LOW PRIORITY
- REQUIRES MORE INVESTMENT OF TIME, MONEY, ETC.
- YIELDS LOW OUTCOME

### HIGH RISK
- REQUIRES SIGNIFICANT INVESTMENT OF TIME, MONEY, CAPITAL, ETC.

# BUSINESS PLAN

Now that you have categorized each idea, let's take it a step further and create a short one-page business plan for each idea.

*This template loosely includes a SWOT (strengths, weaknesses, opportunities, and threats) analysis.*

**IDEA 1**

_____

### PROBLEM
What problem will your business solve?
_____
_____
_____

### SOLUTION
What product/ service will your business provide to solve the problem?
_____
_____

### ADVANTAGE
What will be your unique competitive advantage over your competition? Also list opportunities.
_____
_____

### AUDIENCE
Who will purchase your product or service?
_____
_____
_____

### MODEL
Describe your business model/ how your business will make money.
_____
_____

### ANALYSIS
Who are your competitors? Also include potential risks/threats to the company.
_____
_____

### FUNDING
How much funding will you need to get started? Also, include any weaknesses of the business.
_____
_____

### MARKETING
What marketing channels will you utilize to promote your business?
_____
_____

# BUSINESS PLAN

♡♡♡♡♡♡♡  ♡♡♡♡♡♡♡

### IDEA 2

_____

| **PROBLEM** | **SOLUTION** |
|---|---|
| *What problem will your business solve?* | *What product/ service will your business provide to solve the problem?* |
| **ADVANTAGE** | **AUDIENCE** |
| *What will be your unique competitive advantage over your competition? Also list opportunities.* | *Who will purchase your product or service?* |
| **MODEL** | **ANALYSIS** |
| *Describe your business model/ how your business will make money.* | *Who are your competitors? Also include potential risks/threats to the company.* |
| **FUNDING** | **MARKETING** |
| *How much funding will you need to get started? Also, include any weaknesses of the business.* | *What marketing channels will you utilize to promote your business?* |

# BUSINESS PLAN

♡♡♡♡♡♡♡  ♡♡♡♡♡♡♡

**IDEA 3**

_____

### PROBLEM
*What problem will your business solve?*
_____
_____
_____

### SOLUTION
*What product/ service will your business provide to solve the problem?*
_____
_____
_____

### ADVANTAGE
*What will be your unique competitive advantage over your competition? Also list opportunities.*
_____
_____
_____

### AUDIENCE
*Who will purchase your product or service?*
_____
_____
_____

### MODEL
*Describe your business model/ how your business will make money.*
_____
_____
_____

### ANALYSIS
*Who are your competitors? Also include potential risks/threats to the company.*
_____
_____
_____

### FUNDING
*How much funding will you need to get started? Also, include any weaknesses of the business.*
_____
_____
_____

### MARKETING
*What marketing channels will you utilize to promote your business?*
_____
_____
_____

# BUSINESS PLAN

**IDEA 4**

_____

### PROBLEM
*What problem will your business solve?*
_____
_____
_____

### SOLUTION
*What product/ service will your business provide to solve the problem?*
_____
_____
_____

### ADVANTAGE
*What will be your unique competitive advantage over your competition? Also list opportunities.*
_____
_____
_____

### AUDIENCE
*Who will purchase your product or service?*
_____
_____
_____

### MODEL
*Describe your business model/ how your business will make money.*
_____
_____
_____

### ANALYSIS
*Who are your competitors? Also include potential risks/threats to the company.*
_____
_____
_____

### FUNDING
*How much funding will you need to get started? Also, include any weaknesses of the business.*
_____
_____
_____

### MARKETING
*What marketing channels will you utilize to promote your business?*
_____
_____
_____

# BUSINESS PLAN

**IDEA 5**

_____

### PROBLEM
*What problem will your business solve?*
_____
_____
_____

### SOLUTION
*What product/ service will your business provide to solve the problem?*
_____
_____
_____

### ADVANTAGE
*What will be your unique competitive advantage over your competition? Also list opportunities.*
_____
_____
_____

### AUDIENCE
*Who will purchase your product or service?*
_____
_____
_____

### MODEL
*Describe your business model/ how your business will make money.*
_____
_____
_____

### ANALYSIS
*Who are your competitors? Also include potential risks/threats to the company.*
_____
_____
_____

### FUNDING
*How much funding will you need to get started? Also, include any weaknesses of the business.*
_____
_____
_____

### MARKETING
*What marketing channels will you utilize to promote your business?*
_____
_____
_____

# BUSINESS PLAN

## IDEA 6

_____

### PROBLEM
*What problem will your business solve?*
_____
_____
_____

### SOLUTION
*What product/ service will your business provide to solve the problem?*
_____
_____
_____

### ADVANTAGE
*What will be your unique competitive advantage over your competition? Also list opportunities.*
_____
_____
_____

### AUDIENCE
*Who will purchase your product or service?*
_____
_____
_____

### MODEL
*Describe your business model/ how your business will make money.*
_____
_____

### ANALYSIS
*Who are your competitors? Also include potential risks/threats to the company.*
_____
_____

### FUNDING
*How much funding will you need to get started? Also, include any weaknesses of the business.*
_____
_____

### MARKETING
*What marketing channels will you utilize to promote your business?*
_____
_____

# BUSINESS PLAN

### IDEA 7

_____

### PROBLEM
*What problem will your business solve?*
_____
_____

### SOLUTION
*What product/ service will your business provide to solve the problem?*
_____
_____

### ADVANTAGE
*What will be your unique competitive advantage over your competition? Also list opportunities.*
_____
_____

### AUDIENCE
*Who will purchase your product or service?*
_____
_____

### MODEL
*Describe your business model/ how your business will make money.*
_____
_____

### ANALYSIS
*Who are your competitors? Also include potential risks/threats to the company.*
_____
_____

### FUNDING
*How much funding will you need to get started? Also, include any weaknesses of the business.*
_____
_____

### MARKETING
*What marketing channels will you utilize to promote your business?*
_____
_____

# YOUR BRAND IDENTITY

It's time for the fun part using your top business idea!

## BRAND IDENTITY

# **DEFINING YOUR BRAND**

Defining a strong and memorable brand identity involves developing a narrative and creating elements that clearly represents your business. When creating your brand, consider your brand story, business purpose & values, audience & customer experience and visual content & marketing strategy. Let's define your brand!

### BUSINESS NAME

_____

### BUSINESS TAGLINE

_____

### BUSINESS MISSION STATEMENT/ PITCH

_____

### BUSINESS TONE & VOICE
Will the language behind your brand be sophisticated, carefree, unconventional, etc.

_____

### BUSINESS PERSONALITY
List 3-5 words that describes your brand.

_____

# BRAND IDENTITY

# DESIGNING YOUR BRAND

After you have defined your brand identity, you can begin to design your brand identity. Once you have successfully established your brand identity, you can then create marketing collateral and a website.

## BUSINESS LOGO

*Draft 1*  *Draft 2*

## BUSINESS COLORS

_____   _____   _____

_____   _____   _____

## BUSINESS TYPOGRAPHY/FONTS

_____   _____   _____

## VALUE PROPOSITION

# HOW TO WIN

A good way to attract customers and increase sales is to add value to your business. It is very imperative to consider all touch points of your business when thinking about value. Below are examples of how you can add value to your brand.

**1** Deliver more than what your customer is expecting.

**2** Increase convenience.

**3** Improve customer service and offer ongoing support.

**4** Create loyalty programs.

**5** Build relationships with your customers and personalize customer experience.

**6** Highlight the outcome/ long-term takaways.

# VALUE PROPOSITION

**7.** Create an added brand benefit (start a podcast, teach a class, host an event).

**8.** Share valuable content.

**9.** Engage your audience and encourage audience participation.

**10.** Serve as an industry expert/Advisor to your customers.

**11.** Remove customer fear.

**12.** Collect actionable feedback.

*"Plan your work, then work your plan". -Margaret Thatcher*

*"She who fails to plan is planning to fail"*

Winston Churchill

*If the plan doesn't work, change the plan not the goal*

INCORPORATE YOUR SMALL BUSINESS

# GET LEGAL

# INCORPORATE

## YOUR CHECKLIST

Incorporating your small business is the official way to legally separate you, the owner, from the actual business. There are many benefits to incorporating but the number one reason to incorporate is to protect your personal assets as the business owner.

Any business debts or obligations that the business acquires will be limited to the business entity only. You, the business owner, will have limited liability for any business debt.

Below is a quick checklist to get you started with incorporating your business. Those marked with an asterisk are federal and state requirements. Please research the laws according to your state.

### CHECKLIST

- [ ] Verify your business name
- [ ] Create a business email address
- [ ] Identify a business mailing address
- [ ] Decide how you would like to incorporate
- [ ] Create governing documents and bylaws
- [ ] File appropriate documents with the Secretary of State
- [ ] Apply for a DBA/trade name if needed
- [ ] Apply for an Employer Identification Number (EIN number)*
- [ ] Apply for a business license*
- [ ] Open up a business bank account*
- [ ] Start a small business Records Book

## INCORPORATE

# YOUR CHECKLIST

### VERIFY YOUR BUSINESS NAME

Verify that your business name is not already in use in your state. Visit the Secretary of State to perform a search on business names. If the name is already in use, in your state, then you will have to select a different name. If not, then you can use your respective business name.

### CREATE A BUSINESS EMAIL ADDRESS

I highly recommend using a Google Gmail account. Google offers a lot of services that can benefit you later down the line. Google also offers Gmail for business. Price: $6.00 per month.

### IDENTIFY A BUSINESS MAILING ADDRESS

I highly recommend getting a P.O. Box. You will have to use a personal address when incorporating but the P.O. Box will serve as your business address. Price: Varies depending on state, the size of the box and the length of rental time. Approx price: $75.00 for six months.

### DECIDE HOW YOU WILL INCORPORATE

Please see the next page for a *short* comparison of business entities. Please conduct your own research to see which entity type is best suited for you.

# YOUR CHECKLIST

## ENTITY TYPES

### SOLE PROPRIETOR

Pros
- Easy to establish
- Easy tax filing
- You have full control of the business

Cons
- Single owner means only one decision maker. This can make or break you.
- Personally liable for company's debt.
- Difficulty in establishing presence, getting traction and funding.

Tax Treatment
- A "pass-through" entity which means the entity itself is not taxed. The profits and losses are passed through to the owner.

### LIMITED LIABILITY PARTNERSHIP (LLP)

Pros
- Unlimited number of partners allowed. Other restrictions may apply.
- Partners are not personally liable for debts caused by partner negligence. Note: *This does not apply to an unlimited partnership.*

Cons
- There are some restrictions with forming an LLP in some states.

Tax treatment
- A "pass-through" entity which means the entity itself is not taxed. The profits and losses are passed through to the owners.

# INCORPORATE

# YOUR CHECKLIST

## ENTITY TYPES

**LIMITED LIABILITY COMPANY (LLC)**

Pros:
- Unlimited number of members (owners) allowed
- Members (owners) are not personally liable for debits of LLC.

Cons
- Members are responsible for self-employment tax

Tax treatment
- A "pass-through" entity (unless it elects to be taxed), which means the entity itself is not taxed. The profits and losses are passed through to the owner (s).

**"S" CORPORATION**

Pros:
- Maximum number of shareholders is 100.
- Shareholders are not personally liable for "S" corporation's debts.
- No double taxation

Cons
- Annual fees and compliance requirements.
- Stock/Shareholder restrictions

Tax treatment
- Generally, a "pass-through" entity which means the entity itself is not taxed. The profits and losses are passed through to the shareholders.

**"C" CORPORATION**

Pros
- Unlimited number of shareholders allowed.
- Shareholders are not personally liable for "C" corporation's debts.

Cons
- Double Taxation
- Strict compliance requirements

Tax treatment
- Corporation is taxed and dividends distributed to shareholders are also taxed (double taxation).

## INCORPORATE

# YOUR CHECKLIST

### CREATE GOVERNING DOCUMENTS AND BYLAWS

It is required that you create governing documents for your business. This includes the Articles of Incorporation and identifying the incorporators, directors and/or members where applicable. I also recommend that you create bylaws as well.

### FILE APPROPRIATE DOCUMENTS WITH THE SECRETARY OF STATE

Once you have drafted your governing documents, file them with the Secretary of State. Filing fees can vary. Approx price: $100.00

### APPLY FOR A DBA/TRADE NAME

A DBA (Doing Business As) /trade name is simply the name you want to use as your business. Approx price: $225.00.

### APPLY FOR A EMPLOYER IDENTIFICATION NUMBER (EIN NUMBER)

This is like a "social security number" for your business. Price: Free.

### APPLY FOR A BUSINESS LICENSE

You will need to apply for a business license to operate your business in your state/city/county. Price will vary.

### OPEN UP A BUSINESS BANK ACCOUNT

It is important to keep business transactions separate from your personal transactions so you will need to open up a business account.

### START A SMALL BUSINESS RECORDS BOOK

Since you will be operating a business, you will need to keep records of everything. You can also store your governing documents in this book.

Money, Money, Money

# SMALL BUSINESS STARTUP COSTS

## Common Expenses to Consider

# STARTUP COSTS

## THINGS TO CONSIDER

Although the cost of starting a small business will vary depending on the industry, here are some important costs to consider. Please also carefully research your respective industry to get the most accurate expenses.

### SMALL BUSINESS STARTUP COSTS

<u>Essential Costs</u>

▶ Incorporation, licensing, permits, accounting, etc.
*Approx: $300-$500.*

▶ Equipment
*Will vary depending on the industry.*

▶ Inventory
*Will vary depending on the industry.*

▶ Website host and maintenance
*Approx: $9-$29/per month.*

▶ Shipping, packaging, labels, etc.
*Will vary but approx: $4-$29/per item.*

▶ Taxes
*Will vary but approx: $500-$3000+/per quarter.*

# STARTUP COSTS

## MORE SMALL BUSINESS STARTUP COSTS

### Recurring Costs

**Office space and utilities**
Will vary depending on the industry and if you decide to start an at-home business.

**Office supplies**
$100-$300/per quarter.

**Marketing materials**
Will vary but approx: $100-$300/per quarter.

**Insurance**
Will vary depending on the type of insurance you need.

**Payroll,** *if applicable*
Will vary depending on your hiring needs.

### One-time Cost

**Office furniture and smaller equipment**
Will vary but approx: $500-$3000.

# PRODUCT DEVELOPMENT

## DEVELOPMENT

# PRODUCT DEVELOPMENT

Small businesses typically do not have the funding to support large product development so the responsibility of creating a great product or service will be placed on the owner. Although the elements that go into the different stages of product development will vary, here are a few things to consider. Start by researching your respective market and competitors and then start developing your product/service from there.

Create your own custom lists on the following pages.
*All pages may not apply to you.*

### DEVELOP YOUR PROTOTYPE

Write down your top product/ service that you want to create.

------------------------------------------------------------
------------------------------------------------------------
------------------------------------------------------------

List all of the elements that will go into creating your product or service.

------------------------------------------------------------
------------------------------------------------------------
------------------------------------------------------------
------------------------------------------------------------

# DEVELOPMENT

## SUPPLIER LIST

Below, write down a list of potential suppliers/ vendors.

# DEVELOPMENT

## SERVICES

Below, write down a list of services you will offer. *If applicable.*

# DEVENLOPMENT

## INVENTORY

Below, write down a list of potential products that you will offer.

DEVELOPMENT

# CLIENT INTAKE FORM

If you are providing a service, write down your client list below.

# DEVELOPMENT

## ADDITIONAL LIST

Notes

# DEVELOPMENT

## ADDITIONAL LIST

Notes

## DEVELOPMENT

# DESIGN YOUR PROTOTYPE

Now that you have created a list of all of the elements that are needed to create your product or service, now it is time for you to design a physical prototype. Once you have created a prototype, you will then need to test the prototype.

**NOTES ABOUT PROTOTYPE**

# DEVELOPMENT

## DESIGN YOUR PROTOTYPE

**NOTES**

## DEVELOPMENT

# TEST YOUR PROTOTYPE

Once your prototype is complete, you are now ready to test your product/concept with a small control group. Take note of usability, feedback, customer experience, etc.

**NOTES**

# DEVELOPMENT

## TEST YOUR PROTOTYPE

**NOTES**

# DEVELOPMENT

## SUPPLY AND DEMAND

Once you have finalized your prototype you can start creating actual inventory to sell. If you are trying to estimate your demand, one key metric to use is the feedback from your control group.

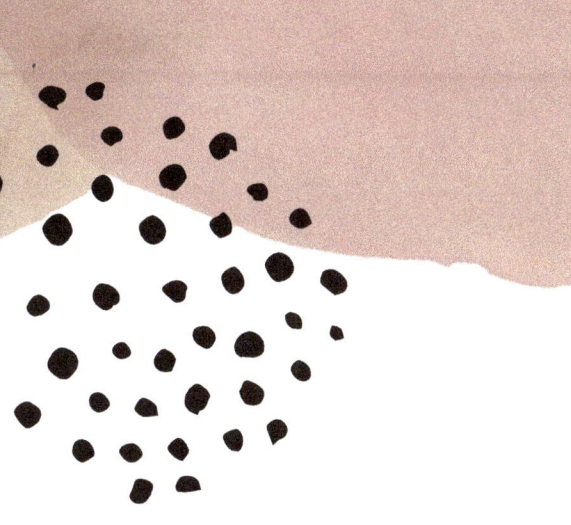

# CREATING POLICIES

for your small business

# POLICIES

## PLACING AN ORDER

Below, write down your order policy. Consider, what will happen if the product is sold out or back-ordered.

# POLICIES

## RETURNS & EXCHANGES

Below, write down your return and exchange policy.

# POLICIES

## SHIPPING

Below, write down your shipping policy. If you will ship internationally, include that below, as a separate policy, as well.

# POLICIES

## CONTRACT

Below, write down any service contracts or agreements between you and potential vendors and/or clients. *If applicable.*

# FORMS

## FOR YOUR SMALL BUSINESS

# FORMS

# INVENTORY MANAGEMENT

Below, write down a list of inventory (final products) and the number you currently have in stock. Use this list to help track your inventory.

# FORMS

# PRICING WORKSHEET

Below, write down a list of your inventory (final products) or service and the total price of each.

# FORMS

## CUSTOMER ORDER FORM

Below, write down orders from your customers.

# FORMS

## CUSTOMER ORDER FORM

# FORMS

## CUSTOMER ORDER FORM

# FORMS

## CUSTOMER ORDER FORM

# SHIPPING TRACKER

Once you receive a customer's order, you will want to keep track of the shipping. Below, write down the shipping information from each order received.

# SHIPPING TRACKER

# FORMS

## SHIPPING TRACKER

# FORMS

## SHIPPING TRACKER

# RETURN TRACKER

Although this does not happen often, it is important to keep track of all returns. Below, write down any returns received.

# PASSWORD TRACKER

Below, write down your username and passwords to your accounts. *Remember to keep this information in a secure place and never share this information with anyone else.*

**OPEN**

**BUSINESS**

*Exceed their expectations*

*Always remember why you started*

—

*Everything you do now is for your future*

—

# PRODUCT LAUNCH TEASER

Once you have created your inventory and have everything in order you are now ready to open for business! *Congratulations*! A great way to get your audience excited about your new product release is to create a marketing teaser campaign. Below, write down a few teaser campaigns to use prior to your launch.

OPEN FOR BUSINESS

# COST STRUCTURE

You have successfully launched your business and orders have started to pour in. Now you want to keep track of all of your sells and any expenses. Remember to review your income and expenses on a continuous basis.

## REVENUE TRACKER

| Date | Customer | Item | Subtotal | Taxes | Total |
|------|----------|------|----------|-------|-------|
|      |          |      |          |       |       |
|      |          |      |          |       |       |
|      |          |      |          |       |       |
|      |          |      |          |       |       |
|      |          |      |          |       |       |

OPEN FOR BUSINESS

# COST STRUCTURE

## REVENUE TRACKER

| Date | Customer | Item | Subtotal | Taxes | Total |
|------|----------|------|----------|-------|-------|
|      |          |      |          |       |       |
|      |          |      |          |       |       |
|      |          |      |          |       |       |
|      |          |      |          |       |       |
|      |          |      |          |       |       |
|      |          |      |          |       |       |

OPEN FOR BUSINESS

# COST STRUCTURE

## EXPENSE TRACKER

| Date | Customer | Item | Subtotal | Taxes | Total |
|------|----------|------|----------|-------|-------|
|      |          |      |          |       |       |
|      |          |      |          |       |       |
|      |          |      |          |       |       |
|      |          |      |          |       |       |
|      |          |      |          |       |       |
|      |          |      |          |       |       |

OPEN FOR BUSINESS

# COST STRUCTURE

## EXPENSE TRACKER

| Date | Customer | Item | Subtotal | Taxes | Total |
|---|---|---|---|---|---|
|  |  |  |  |  |  |
|  |  |  |  |  |  |
|  |  |  |  |  |  |
|  |  |  |  |  |  |
|  |  |  |  |  |  |
|  |  |  |  |  |  |

OPEN FOR BUSINESS

# COST STRUCTURE

## BILL TRACKER

| Date | Customer | Item | Subtotal | Taxes | Total |
|------|----------|------|----------|-------|-------|
|      |          |      |          |       |       |
|      |          |      |          |       |       |
|      |          |      |          |       |       |
|      |          |      |          |       |       |
|      |          |      |          |       |       |
|      |          |      |          |       |       |

OPEN FOR BUSINESS

# COST STRUCTURE

## BILL TRACKER

| Date | Customer | Item | Subtotal | Taxes | Total |
|------|----------|------|----------|-------|-------|
|      |          |      |          |       |       |
|      |          |      |          |       |       |
|      |          |      |          |       |       |
|      |          |      |          |       |       |
|      |          |      |          |       |       |
|      |          |      |          |       |       |

OPEN FOR BUSINESS

# COST STRUCTURE

## TAX PAYMENT TRACKER

| Date | Customer | Item | Subtotal | Taxes | Total |
|------|----------|------|----------|-------|-------|
|      |          |      |          |       |       |
|      |          |      |          |       |       |
|      |          |      |          |       |       |
|      |          |      |          |       |       |
|      |          |      |          |       |       |
|      |          |      |          |       |       |

OPEN FOR BUSINESS

# COST STRUCTURE

## TAX PAYMENT TRACKER

| Date | Customer | Item | Subtotal | Taxes | Total |
|------|----------|------|----------|-------|-------|
|      |          |      |          |       |       |
|      |          |      |          |       |       |
|      |          |      |          |       |       |
|      |          |      |          |       |       |
|      |          |      |          |       |       |
|      |          |      |          |       |       |

OPEN FOR BUSINESS

# COUPONS AND DISCOUNTS

Track any coupons or discounts for customers below.

| | CODE | %OFF | EFFECTIVE DATES |
|---|---|---|---|
| COUPON 1 | | | |
| COUPON 2 | | | |
| COUPON 3 | | | |
| COUPON 4 | | | |
| COUPON 5 | | | |
| COUPON 6 | | | |
| COUPON 7 | | | |

# KEY METRICS

As you begin to develop your business, it is imperative to keep track of key metrics to measure business performance, Things to consider are sales revenue, customer retention rate, website traffic, etc.

OPEN FOR BUSINESS

# KEY METRICS

## MILESTONES

Once you determine your performance metrics and how you will measure business success,, you can then set milestones. This can serve as a road map for your business. Examples include, achieving a certain amount of sells by a specific date, staying within a certain budget, etc.

OPEN FOR BUSINESS

# MILESTONES

# SOCIAL MEDIA TRACKER

Using social media to market your product or service is a great way to grow your business. Use the space below to track hashtags, keywords and create a schedule. Remember to keep it simple and engaging.

## HASHTAG TRACKER

## KEYWORD TRACKER

OPEN FOR BUSINESS

# SOCIAL MEDIA TRACKER

| | PLATFORM | CONTENT | TIME | STATS |
|---|---|---|---|---|
| SUNDAY | | | | |
| MONDAY | | | | |
| TUESDAY | | | | |
| WEDNESDAY | | | | |
| THURSDAY | | | | |
| FRIDAY | | | | |
| SATURDAY | | | | |

OPEN FOR BUSINESS

# SOCIAL MEDIA TRACKER

| | PLATFORM | CONTENT | TIME | STATS |
|---|---|---|---|---|
| SUNDAY | | | | |
| MONDAY | | | | |
| TUESDAY | | | | |
| WEDNESDAY | | | | |
| THURSDAY | | | | |
| FRIDAY | | | | |
| SATURDAY | | | | |

# OPEN FOR BUSINESS

## PAUSE AND REVIEW

Now that you have your performance metrics and milestones in place, it is important to review your business operations often to see what can be improved, changed or updated.

**NOTES**

# GROWTH STAGE

> "We cannot become what we want by remaining what we are"
>
> — Max De Pree

*Continue to grow and evolve*

*Remember if you play small you stay small*

## GROWTH STAGE

# LOOKING AHEAD

It is never too earlier to create a 5-year strategic plan for your business. Although your business may still be in the beginning stage, by now, you should have developed an idea of where you want your business to go. Below create a 3-5 year plan for your business.

### YEAR 1-3

## GROWTH STAGE

# LOOKING AHEAD

**YEAR 4-5**

# THE CEO CLUB

# PROFESSIONAL GROUPS

It is official! You have now entered into the prestigious CEO club. Because everyone in your circle will not understand the challenges and successes that you will experience while on your entrepreneurial journey, it is important to find supportive professional and networking groups. Research local groups then write down the groups that will be best suited for you.

**NETWORKS GROUPS**

**PROFESSIONAL ASSOCIATIONS**

# RESOURCES

As a new small business, the process of getting started can seem a bit overwhelming but I am here to help.  Below is a *short* list of additional resources to help get you started.  In addition, I offer this list for those who would like to utilize digital platforms.

### E-commerce Platforms
- Shopify
- WooCommerce
- Magento
- BigCommerce
- SquareSpace
- Etsy

### Email Marketing
- Constant Contact
- Mailchimp
- Twilio
- Drip

### Social Media Management
- Buffer
- Hootsuite
- Sprout Social
- Sendible

### Bookkeeping
- Wave Accounting
- FreshBooks
- Xero
- Quickbooks Self-Employed

### Platforms for Creators/Crafters
- Craftybase
- SoapMaker

### Bonus - Books
- StrengthsFinders 2.0
- In the Company of Women

# GOOD LUCK!

Ladies, we are the next generation of leaders and there is so much opportunity for us to get in this game and WIN!

Get creative with your ideas, do your research and most importantly, don't give up!

Wishing you all the best.

*Sincerely, Angie* ♥

# TAKE NOTES

USE THE NEXT SECTION TO TAKE ANY ADDITIONAL NOTES

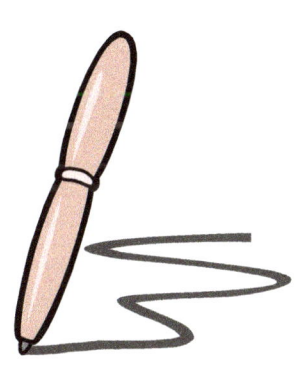

# NOTES

## ADDITIONAL INFORMATION

# NOTES

## ADDITIONAL INFORMATION

# ADDITIONAL INFORMATION

# NOTES

## ADDITIONAL INFORMATION

# NOTES

## ADDITIONAL INFORMATION

# NOTES

## ADDITIONAL INFORMATION

NOTES

# TASK TRACKER

Keep track of your business tasks below.

**TASK** | **NOTES**

**URGENCY** | **COMPLETE**

TASK | NOTES

URGENCY | COMPLETE

**TASK** | **NOTES**

**URGENCY** | **COMPLETE**

TASK | NOTES

URGENCY | COMPLETE

NOTES

# TASK TRACKER

Keep track of your business tasks below.

| TASK | NOTES |
|------|-------|
| URGENCY | COMPLETE |
| TASK | NOTES |
| URGENCY | COMPLETE |
| TASK | NOTES |
| URGENCY | COMPLETE |
| TASK | NOTES |
| URGENCY | COMPLETE |

NOTES

# TASK TRACKER

Keep track of your business tasks below.

**TASK**  **NOTES**

**URGENCY**  **COMPLETE**

TASK  NOTES

URGENCY  COMPLETE

**TASK**  **NOTES**

**URGENCY**  **COMPLETE**

TASK  NOTES

URGENCY  COMPLETE

NOTES

# TASK TRACKER

Keep track of your business tasks below.

**TASK** — **NOTES**

**URGENCY** — **COMPLETE**

TASK — NOTES

URGENCY — COMPLETE

**TASK** — **NOTES**

**URGENCY** — **COMPLETE**

TASK — NOTES

URGENCY — COMPLETE